Super B[...]
Howling Bucket

written and illustrated by

Matthew Urmenyhazi

Harcourt Achieve

Rigby • Saxon • Steck-Vaughn

www.HarcourtAchieve.com
1.800.531.5015

Characters

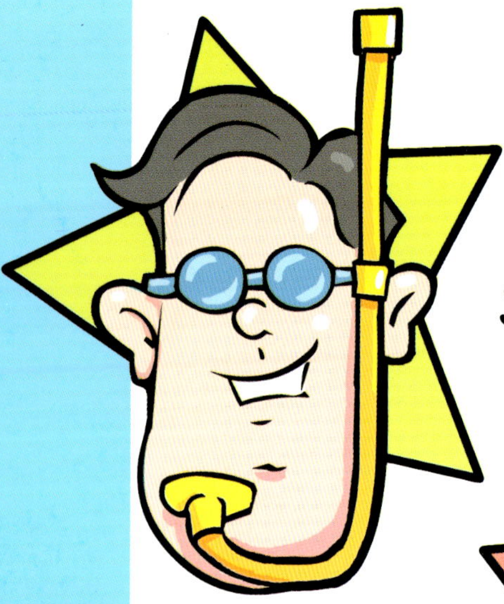

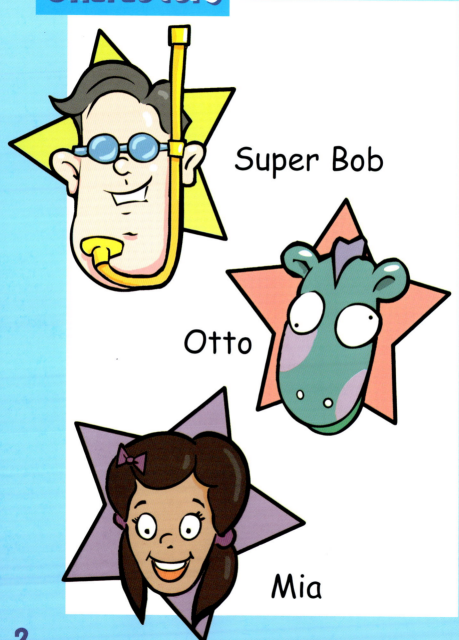

Super Bob

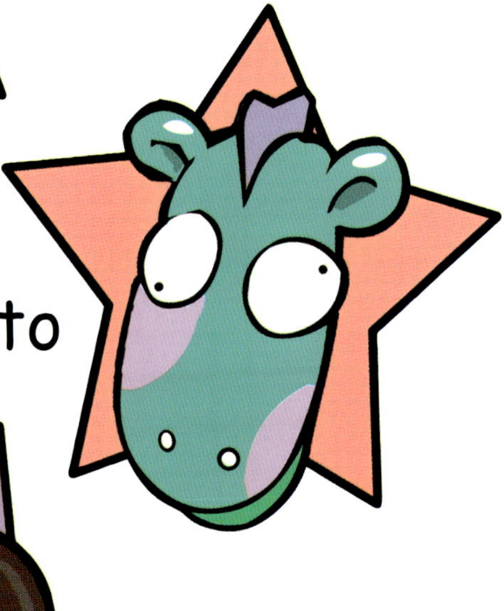

Otto

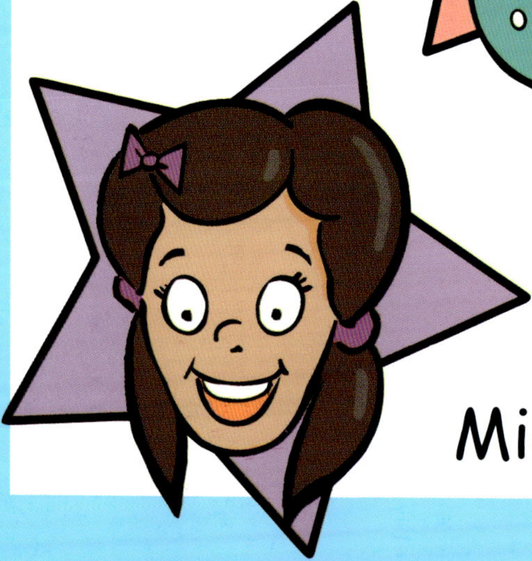

Mia

Contents

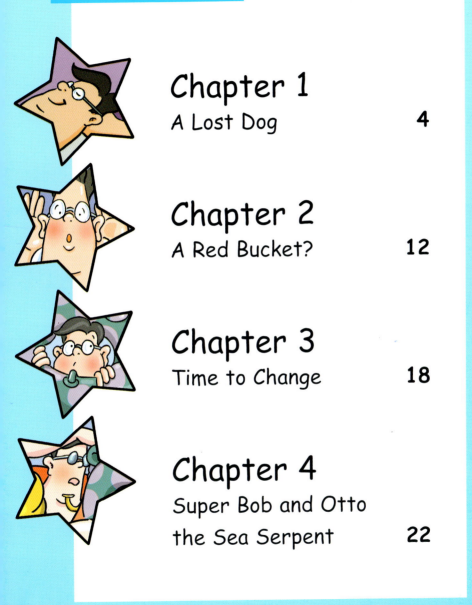

Chapter 1

A Lost Dog

"Ahh," Bob thought to himself, "another glorious day!" He propped his head upon his arms and sank into a deep, deep sleep.

Bob dreamed about a wonderful day. It was just like this one, but with cakes and sweets and fizzy drinks.

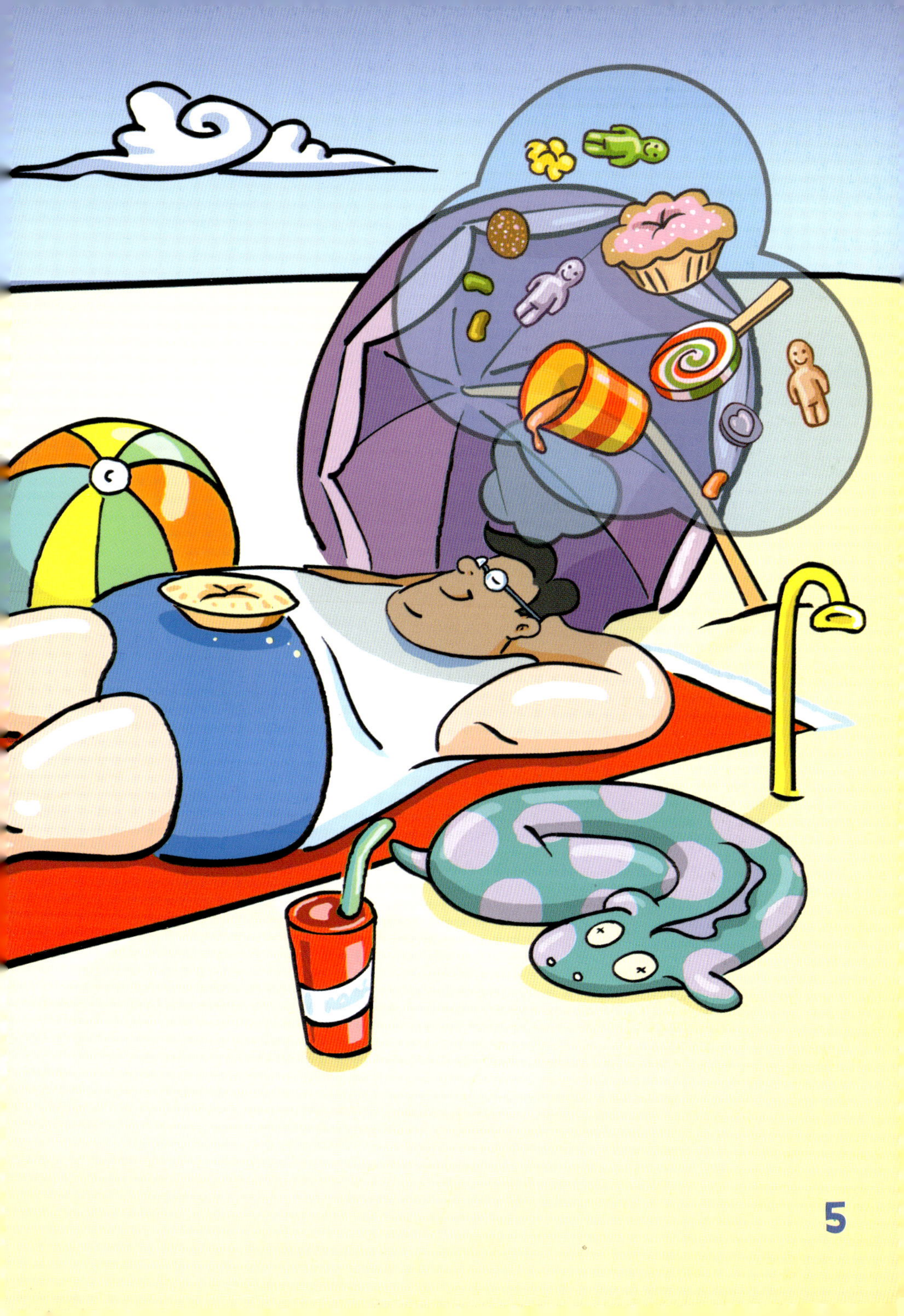

Bob loved birds, which meant
he loved seagulls. As Bob dozed,
he kept one eye open to watch
them feed.

6

The seagulls would tickle his tummy as they pecked at his apple pie.

Suddenly Bob was woken from his nap.

"My name is Mia, and I've lost my dog," cried a little girl with pigtails. "Have you seen him? His name is Nugget! He has spots, a white tail, and sore ears."

Bob slowly lifted his sleepy head. He tried to remember what the little girl had said. "Sore ears, spots . . . and chicken nuggets, did you say?"

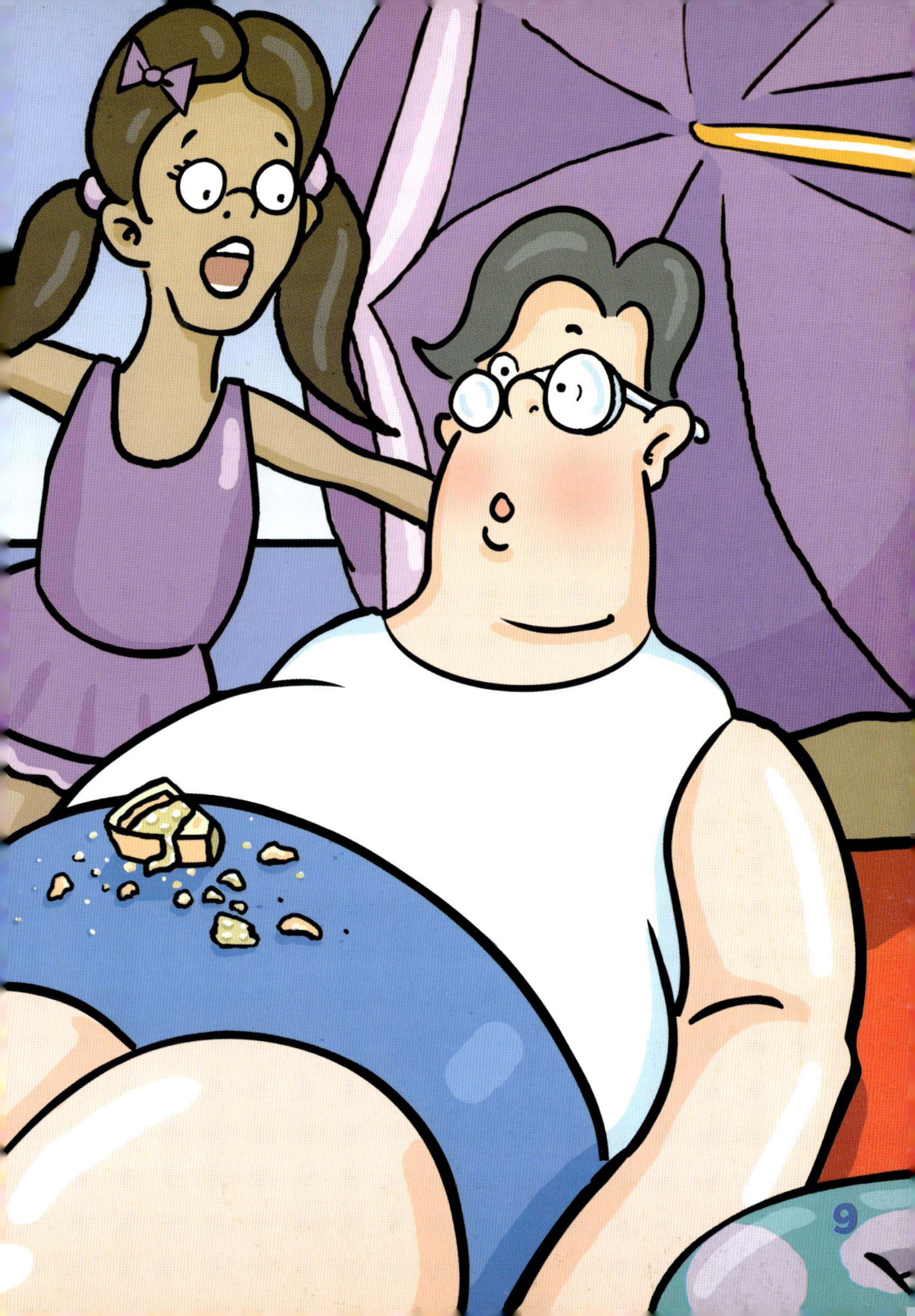

"I was in the middle of a dream. It was about cream cakes and ice creams and candy and oh, um, err . . . zzz."

Bob's eyes became heavy. He began to snooze again. Mia ran off to find someone a bit more helpful.

Chapter 2

A Red Bucket?

Suddenly shouts and screams filled the air.
Bob sat up quickly.

Now he was really awake!

Everyone was running out of the water.
They were all pointing at something out
in the deep blue water. An eerie sound
filled the air.

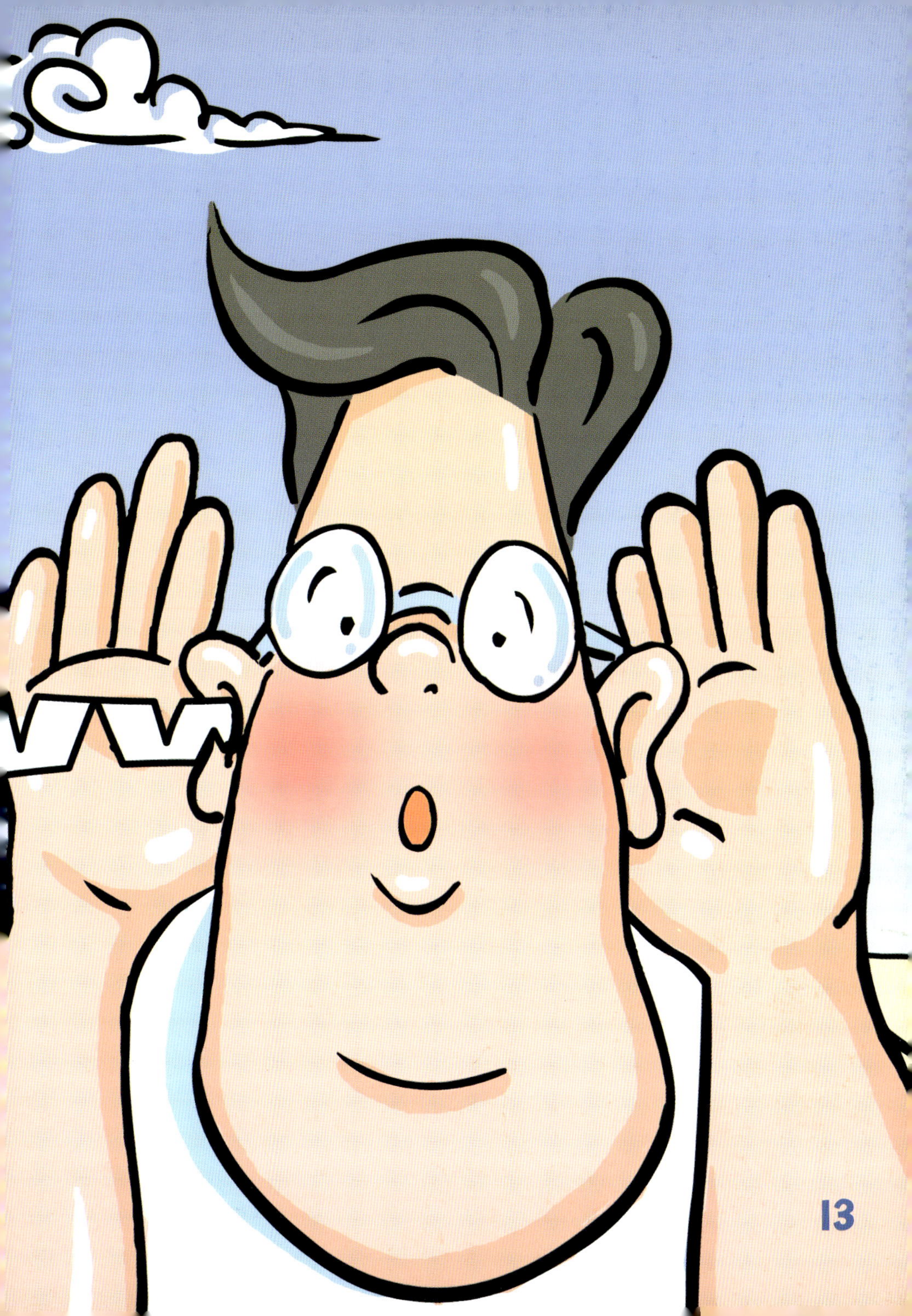

It seemed to be coming from . . .
a red bucket?

It was bobbing up and down and heading out to sea.

"Hmmm. What a funny sight to see," thought Bob to himself.

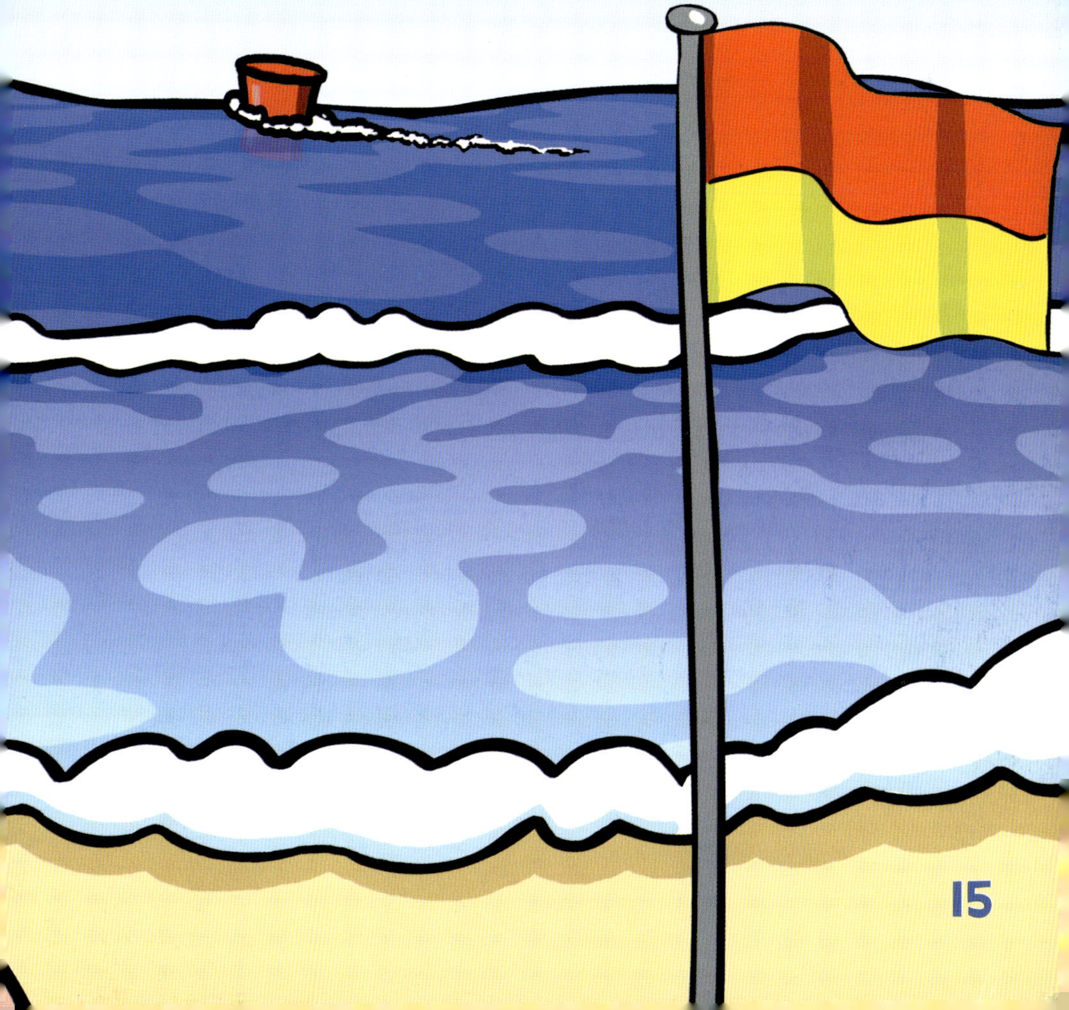

A sickening howl came from the bucket.

"Come on, Otto, old buddy," said Bob.
"We have a mystery to solve."

Chapter 3

Time to Change

Bob puffed away. Slowly Otto grew into a large and happy sea serpent. Otto had never been too keen on getting into deep water. He was happy to stay in shallow water.

"I'll just slip into my gear," said Bob.
"I'll squeeze this arm through here.
Now I'll turn around a bit . . . "

Bob was always ready for action and
adventure. He just needed time to get
changed first.

Bob was almost ready. He added his goggles and breathing tube, his floaties and flippers, and, of course, his trusty towel.

Bob and Otto suddenly became . . .

Chapter 4

Super Bob and Otto the Sea Serpent

It was time to head out to sea. It was time to solve the mystery of the howling bucket.

At first the water was calm and shallow. But the waves grew bigger. It was getting dangerous.

"Full steam ahead," Bob urged Otto. Without saying a word, Otto pushed them both over the waves.

"Phew!" They finally made it past the breaking waves. "Good for you, Otto. You're a trusty old sea snake!" said Super Bob.

Poor Otto didn't say a thing. He was pretty tired. He was also happy to be out of danger — for now.

"Ooooaaawww!" The howl was louder now. The red bucket drifted toward them.

Super Bob trembled. He slowly peered over the edge of the bucket.

"A dog?" laughed Super Bob. "You must be the spotted Nugget with sore ears and a white tail."

"Oooowww," said the little dog. He was so dog-tired.

Super Bob scooped the dog up. "OK, Otto,
back to shore, and make it snappy!" Otto's
head bobbed a bit as he carried them into
the shore.

27

"Nugget!" cried the little girl. "You're safe!"
She hugged the two superheroes.

"Thank you so much, Super Bob and Otto.
You're my heroes!"

"All in a day's work," replied Super Bob. "If there's a mystery to solve, or an adventure to be had, we'll be there!"

Otto sat and stared, as he often did. All he said was, "Pffffttt."

Glossary

drifting
being carried by water

eerie
strange and scary

mystery
something strange and unknown

peered
looked carefully

shallow
water that is not deep

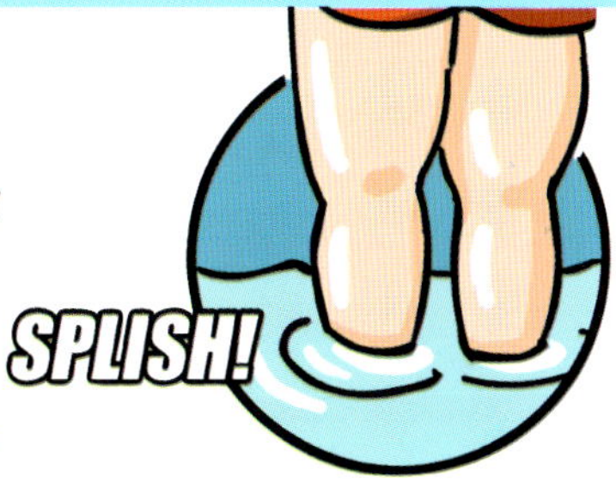
SPLISH!

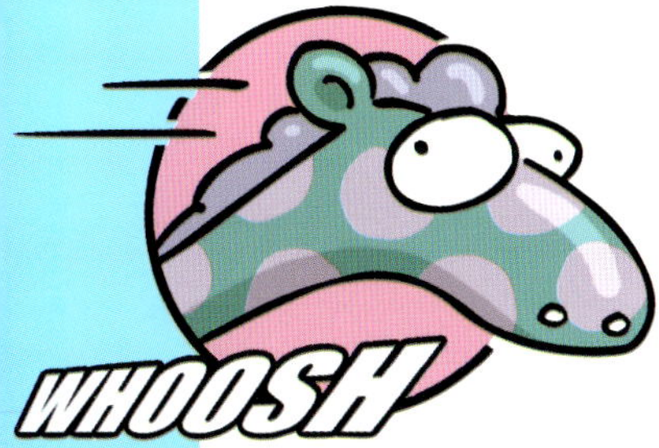
WHOOSH

snappy
quick

snooze
a short, light sleep

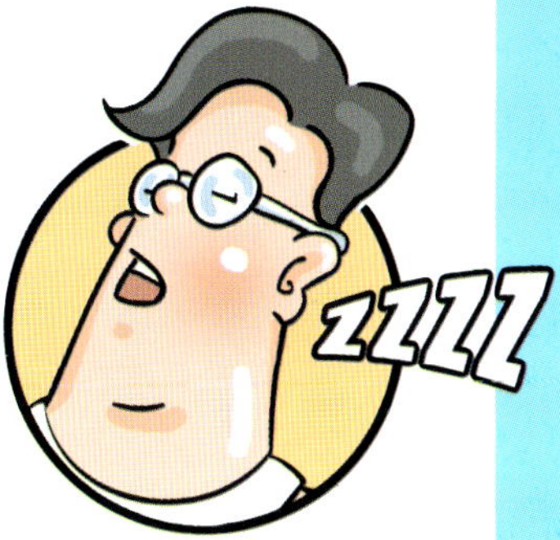
ZZZZ

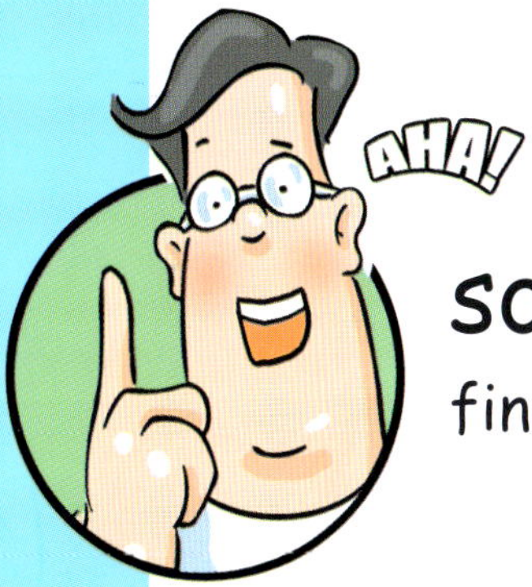
AHA!

solve
find an answer

Matthew Urmenyhazi

Hiding inside this book is this secret sea snail. Can you find him?

Matthew Urmenyhazi wanted to grow up to be a mad scientist. He thought mad scientists could turn chickens into frogs.

Now Matthew has grown up. He spends most of his time on a computer doing special effects for film and television. He can make people walk and talk in slow motion and then make them disappear. He can even make lightning bolts, but he is still trying to turn a chicken into a frog.